The Journey

A Relentless Effort to Spread Motivation to the World

 KNOWLEDGE POWER BOOKS • VALENCIA, CA 91355

Copyright by Denesha Degraffenreid

All rights reserved. In accordance with the U.S. Copyright Act of 1976, the scanning, uploading, and electronic sharing of any part of this book without the permission of the publisher is unlawful piracy ad theft of the author's intellectual property. If you would like to use material from this book (other than for review purposes), prior written permission must be obtained by contacting the publisher at info@knowledgepowerinc.com

Thank you for your support of the author's rights.

ISBN: 978-0-9993455-3-5
Library of Congress Control Number: 2017953996

Edited by: Laurel J. Davis
Cover Design: Juan Roberts, Creative Lunacy, Inc.
Literary Director: Sandra L. Slayton

Published by:

Knowledge Power Books
A Division of Knowledge Power Communications, Inc.
Valencia, CA 91355
www.knowledgepowerbooks.com

Printed in the United States of America

Dedication

This book is dedicated to the memory of my late
Grandmother Mamie K. McFadden.
*Although you're gone your memories and life lessons will
forever live on. Especially in this book of poems.*

Thank You,
-Nesha

Contents

Dedication	iii
Collection of Poems	
Dreaming	1
Striving	3
War	5
Just Thinkin'	6
Over Thinkin'	8
Be	11
Black Girl Lost	12
Stand	14
Surroundings	17
Have You Ever?	19
Moving or Standing?	21
Just a Thought	23

Kindred Spirit and a Friend	25
Give Thanks	27
Is It You?	29
Mrs. Wrong	31
Message	33
Umbrella	34
What are We Waiting For?	36
Can You Only Imagine?	38
Still Dreaming	41
Willingness or Willing-less?	43
A Teaspoon of Motivation	45
Just Think About It	46
Destined	47
Driven	48
A Poem of Small Quotes	49
A Small Prayer	50
Mentorship	51
Shepherd's Tree	52
For the Love of Music	53
Finding Happiness in the Joke	55
Fear, Guilt, and Shame	57
Searching for What's Present	59

THE JOURNEY

Vulnerability	61
Am I?	63
Don't Quit	65
Gazing	67
Question	68
Choices	70
Just Think	72
Change	74
Complaints	75
Thoughts	77
The Love From a Woman	80
About the Author	83

Dreaming

A DREAM IS BUT A DREAM. THEY ALWAYS FEEL REAL.

Hope is just a feeling which many people give.

Love is an emotion, sometimes abused.

Love is an emotion, not an excuse.

Consistency is key. It'll unlock many doors.

Don't contain bravery, especially if it's yours.

The truth is exactly that: you give it, you get it back.

Sometimes . . .

Teasing isn't a fair action. It causes actions to be blind.

A dream is but a dream. Is it ever real?

Hope is an action; don't take just to give.

Love is a feeling; it's pleasurable to have.

Consistency is bravery.

Does it have to be in arm's reach, in order to be grabbed?

Tell the truth about what seems.

Love yourself. Make life your dream.

Striving

ALL I EVER WANTED WAS TO MAKE YOU HAPPY. ALL I EVER WANTED WAS TO MAKE YOU PROUD.

I cannot believe the words that I am hearing from you right now.

I've worked so diligently over the years, to please you and only you.

You were always there for me to come to.

You lifted me up the many times I've dropped to my knees and cried.

You've been my bright eyes the many times I was lost and blind.

I've shared with you my entire life story. The good and the bad, and you told me do not worry.

You've been my legs when I couldn't stand. Just so you know, that was never a part of my plan.

You've given me a hand up when I thought everything was smooth sailing.

You've been here for me even when everyone else was bailing.

So many times I've cried and you've wiped my tears.

You've patiently watched me grow over the years.

I can't think of one time you've actually said no, no matter how hard I try.

You were the one who taught me: it's see you later, not goodbye.

I'll always have your presence in my memory,
Since I know no more will you be here with me.

All I ever wanted was to make you happy. All I ever wanted was to make you proud.

Now your face is like another stranger I bypass in a large crowd.

War

ALL I EVER WANTED WAS EQUALITY AND PEACE.

Forget about me.

Remember war on poverty.

War on drugs.

War on violence

What about war on injustice?

War on you and war on me?

War on hate crimes.

War on gangs.

War on victims, they're not the ones to blame.

Just Thinkin'

As I sit on my bed and I think about life,

I think about the pain and I think about the strife.

I think about the joy and I think about the gain.

I think about the sunny days and the many days it rained.

I think about the beautiful smile of my mother.

I think about the stern but loving voice of my dad.

I think about my family as a whole and all the caring times we've had.

I think about the trying times, too. But God was always there to pull us through.

Remembering my grandmother in her last days.

Jesus, you know we all need you to lift us up. Only to you I pray.

I oftentimes sit in silence and listen to my surroundings.

THE JOURNEY

When it's very quiet, the energy is always so loud.

Trying to uplift everyone who may be feeling down.

The presence of God is always around.

We're living . . . Everything is unknown . . . God, watch us, until the day you welcome us into your throne.

Over Thinkin'

As I stare at this blank paper. I'm scrambling for the words to write.

I pray to God that he'll bless my tongue, and my mind, so I'll be able to type.

There's something greater that lies within us all.

Often times we are our own downfall.

Wanting everything immediately, instead of enjoying the wait.

Sometimes in this life it narrows down to give or take.

Not in a criminal way, but maybe my neighbor has something I need.

Sit down and really think about it: Everyone on this planet needs the trees to breathe.

Without them the good "air" would be no more.

THE JOURNEY

Look around the world at all the infrastructure.

So many buildings being built, as if planet earth is growing.

When will it end? Trees are being cut down. Think about it again.

We all want so much, but want to give so little. It shouldn't take this much to be pleased.

Once upon a time, in the beginning, people weren't so in need.

In need of physical things when true happiness lies within.

I pray that everyone finds this time and time again.

Gardening, farming, and enjoying the great outdoors.

Children honoring their parents, even children playing with toys.

Technology sometimes I think is a living thing. It possesses the minds of many.

It has changed many people to where they aren't so friendly.

Some sit inside all day rarely making human connection.

God blessed us with a tongue to speak and to give others direction.

As I stare at the words on this paper, I realize I'm writing in hopes of finding the truth.

I pray to God he'll bless me with it, in hopes it'll then bless you.

Be

BE THE ONE TO STAND OUT.

Be the rain, in the middle of a drought.

Be the change you want to see.

Be the change you see in me.

Be the change you see in the world.

Be the change that doesn't cause turmoil.

Be the change you have yet to understand.

Be the change you see that sets a part of God's plan.

Be the change, not the dollar.

Be the leader instead of the follower.

Be the change, that'll change CHANGE.

Be the change; show the world everyone isn't the same.

Black Girl Lost

Black girl lost, where am I to go

Black girl lost, I have no soul

Black girl lost, I wish I could find me

Black girl lost, my eyes are wide open and I still cannot see

Black girl lost, my mom is so afraid

Black girl lost, my dad calls every day and says, "I've prayed"

Black girl lost, my brother keeps telling himself this can't be

Black girl lost, why is everyone so concerned

Black girl lost, I'm 25 and I still haven't learned

Black girl lost, my life is going downhill

Black girl lost, I don't even have a purpose to live

THE JOURNEY

Black girl lost, I don't know how I got here

Black girl lost, everyday I'm living in fear

Black girl lost, God I need you here

If you hear me, I'm begging you

If you hear me, where am I to go to?

I'm just a black girl lost

Stand

EVERYONE WANTS TO FIT IN, EVEN WHEN IT'S NOT RIGHT.

No one wants to stand up, no one wants to fight.

Fight for the injustice, and all of the wrong.

Fight for the families whose soldiers didn't come home.

Fight for the debt college students are in.

Fight for the prisoners treated wrong in the pen . . . *they're humans too*

What if you were imprisoned for your mistakes, what would you do?

If you were locked up, would you want to be treated Wrong, too?

Fight for the people suffering from depression.

THE JOURNEY

Fight for people suffering from cancer, who may feel aggression.

Fight for the mothers who just lost their babies . . . *from America, Germany, and even Haiti.*

Fight for love, justice, humility, and peace.

Fight for the homeless person laying out on the streets.

Fight for the teachers who are underpaid;

That teacher fights to educate your child all day while they misbehave.

Fight for the families whose parents are unemployed.

Fight for the men, women, girls, and boys.

Fight for equality, which may lead to better opportunities.

Fight for every single impoverished community.

Fight for equal rights while you're still breathing.

Fight for the cause, it's going to be a change
this season.

Fight for the truth, because so much is wrong.

Fight for the hope that the "lost" people will
come home.

Fight for the child who just lost a parent.

Fight for love, because hate is so apparent.

Fight for everyone, don't try to fit in.

Fight just to fight . . . Maybe someone will listen . . .

Surroundings

MEETING ME IN THE MIDDLE OF NOWHERE. WHERE SHOULD I GO?

Meeting me at the bottom. The end is subzero.

I'm lost. No hope. No soul.

Living amongst liars, cheaters, and thieves.

Living in an environment of disbelief.

Gossip everywhere around me.

I can't escape it. They yearn for it, as if it were the trees.

If they can't gossip, they have no conversation.

I try to be mellow, but it's weighing on my patience.

They ask, what's wrong with you? when I'm not speaking.

Their ears are always open . . . I think they even creep while they sleep.

They make you feel as if you're crazy for not talking about thethings they do

They push you until your back's against the wall and there isnowhere to turn too.

Meeting me in the middle and insanity is what they'll claim.

If I never speak again, my conscious will be to blame.

Have You Ever?

HAVE YOU EVER ATTEMPTED TO BE YOURSELF?

In situations where you understood you were being someone else?

Not speaking when your intuition told you to,

Or speaking when you knew it really wasn't you?

Have you ever gossiped about things that do not concern you?

And look around in the room and wonder who else is Gossiping, too?

Worrying about the wrong things . . .

So caught up in the world, you forgot how to dream?

When was the last time you gave 100 percent?

Went out and made a purchase and thought, hmm, that was money well spent?

Focused on one task at time?

Turned your eyes away from evil as if you were blind?

Ignored a negative comment and continued on with your day?

Didn't feel the urge to reply or have anything to say?

When was the last full week you didn't complain?

Thinking of trying times and blessings as one in the Same?

Have you ever thought what it would be like if the entire world gave their full potential?

Give credit when it's due, and where it's due, and who it's due to?

Have you attempted to be the person you see in the mirror?

No denial, no ignoring, just trying to see the image clearer?

Or are you denying the image in the mirror?

Moving or Standing?

HOW FAR ARE YOU WILLING TO GO TO REACH YOUR DREAMS?

Have you already given up?

Just because you were pushed down, did you not get back up?

When your back was against the wall . . . did you stumble and fall?

In the darkest hours when no one was there . . .

Did you scream to the top your lungs or stand quietly with a blank stare?

When people made up things about you, did you believe it?

When the odds were against you, did you believe you could achieve it?

If the chance was one in five million, do you believe you could receive it?

Do you believe in things that are unseen? If not, you don't have to go anywhere to reach your dreams.

Just a Thought

KEEP PUSHING FORWARD, EVEN WHEN THERE'S A HURRICANE PUSHING YOU BACK.

Don't give up on today, even if you have to pull someone else's slack.

Always remember to smile, even when there's a million things on your brain.

Always remember to love, never let "hate" be the blame.

Everyday isn't going to be a good day, don't be naive to think

That doesn't mean the bad should weigh you down.

How many pounds

Would you put on; just think:. If time tells you, okay, you have no more left,

How would you want to spend your last breath?

Growth is coming in the new year. Make your time now, even if you have to repeat it

To yourself: this year is for me, me, me! Say it. Breathe it.

Believe it!

Kindred Spirit and a Friend

THE DAY I MET YOU, IT ALL MADE SENSE.

You're my kindred spirit; our relationship quickly became intense.

I love the fact you're trying to find you.

I love the fact for your daughter, you're doing what you have to.

I love the fact you're searching for free.

I want you to know you're also helping me find me.

The love we have for poetry, and your hands blessing my hair.

You've introduced me to people I never knew were there.

Your love for art makes you unique.

I know that one day you're going to create a masterpiece.

Always remember your calling.

Give Thanks

AFTER A LONG HARD WEEK AT WORK,

Look up and thank God you've got a job.

After you've spent your entire paycheck on bills,

Look up and thank God for giving you a chance to earn an income.

After a tough argument you've had with your spouse,

Look up and thank God he's blessed you with marriage.

After your child has worked your last nerve,

Look up and thank God for your child.

After you've tried, and tried, and tried . . .

Look up and thank God for giving you the will and the strength to carry on.

After you've done all you can do,

Look up and praise God he instilled the "fight" in you.

Often times we forget, the very things that place us in disarray are the very things that others pray they had or wish they'll get.

Don't mistake your blessings as downfalls or mishaps.

Think about the times you've prayed those very things would exist.

Look after your blessings even once you receive them . . .

Is It You?

THERE'S NOTHING LIKE A GOD-FEARING, HARDWORKING, TRUTH-SEEKING MAN WITH A PLAN:

A man who knows where he's headed, because he knows where he's already been.

A man who doesn't have to speak, but his presence lets you know it's him.

A man who's going through the rain and still isn't wet;

A man who isn't afraid to admit that sometimes he gets upset.

A man who walk the streets, but don't live in 'em;

A man who may be behind bars mentally, but physically don't live in 'em.

There's nothing like a man who takes a stand, but it is still sitting.

Be careful around him: he speaks with intelligence and sometimes you may miss him,

Even when he's there. There's nothing like a man who follows his dream,

Even after time told him things aren't what they seem.

A man who still fights the battle, when his enemy has a Tsar Bomba and all he has are a few pieces of gravel.

A man who knows he's a small section to a big puzzle, and guards negative energy like an animal with a muzzle.

There's nothing like a man who's been pushed against the wall: Looked around, saw devils and said, it's okay, I'll crawl.

A man who knows a blessing is on the way. A man who's building a kingdom in God's way.

Mrs. Wrong

PLEASE LEAVE ME ALONE.

I'm tired of singing the same old song.

Leave me on the corner, I'll be homeless. I'd rather have nowhere to go than be with you and have no hope.

You've made me bitter, and you've stolen my joy.

Mrs. Wrong, I don't won't you anymore.

You altered my thoughts, and made me smile at evil things. You've turned all of my daydreams into wicked things.

Mrs. Wrong, you've made my life a nightmare. You were turning my heart cold.

You almost made me fall in love with gold and the riches it brings. I became obsessed with chasing after designer things, and had feelings of needing diamond rings.

Mrs. Wrong, I'm leaving you. God has a plan for me that doesn't involve you.

Message

Today I received a speeding ticket for speeding through life.

Today I prayed for better days away from the pain and the strife.

Today I tried to receive the message God has for me.

Today someone committed suicide because they were blinded by the darkness and could not see.

Today I don't know what the world is coming to.

Today I prayed for yesterday and the day after, too.

A simple "Hey" could take the pain away!

A simple "Hello" could brighten someone's day!

A simple "Hi" could wipe the tears aside!

Just because it's sweet doesn't mean it's for you.

Just because it's a monkey doesn't mean it belongs at the zoo.

Umbrella

Don't rain on my parade, my life is already dark.

I've always been in the shade, weary days never seem to fade.

So afraid to stand up, because I didn't want to stand out.

So before I let you rain, I'll experience a drought.

Not being selfish, just being true.

You're the very same person who told me one plus one doesn't equal two.

You explained to me that one plus one equals one plus one and that the true equation could never be done.

So I spent hours searching, trying to find my way . . .

THE JOURNEY

I kept the hope, because I knew I'd solve it one day.

A day when the person I looked at in the mirror wouldn't stop me.

ME, YOU won't rain on my parade! God's got me!

What are We Waiting For?

So many times we tell ourselves we cannot do something, even before we try.

As soon as we meet someone, we're already saying goodbye.

We misjudge people by past actions, as if we've made no mistakes.

We give half the effort and then say, I've given it my all; that's all I can take.

So quick to assume that someone will never change.

Play about serious matters as if life is a game.

Never thinking for one second that we are the ones to blame.

THE JOURNEY

Embrace everyone, even the lame.

It'll be then we'll see a real change.

Live limitlessly, today is the day to begin! Today is the day your journey begins!

Can You Only Imagine?

Sometimes it's not about the you, the me, the I, or the we. Sometimes it's about the community.

Imagine the entire world coming together as one. Everyone being treated equal. That would really get the job done.

Imagine a world when -- and if we need help, we could just call on our neighbor, with no judgment being cast upon us.

Could you imagine a world filled with epidemic peace? A world where love fills the streets instead of fraud and worries of disbelief?

Imagine a world where all starving children are fed, children have both parents to tuck them in bed. Both parents there to read bedtime stories at night.

THE JOURNEY

Imagine a world where politics, war and money aren't placed before a human life. Could you imagine what that would be like?

A world where people aren't judged by the color of their skin or the area of town they were raised up in. Could you try to imagine such a thing? A world where everyone stand a chance to live out their dreams.

A world where hypocrites don't make things worse than what they seem.

A world with minimal hatred, and people in the workplace get along. Imagine a world where we all would uplift one another. Could you imagine the lyrics to that song?

Imagine a world where people aren't so quick to judge, and take a second to think about what their action actually does. A world where people Don't assume. A world where "higher ups" really consider the grassroots point of view.

A world where jealousy doesn't exist, and fidelity replaces it (*jealously*). A world where everyone pushes to be the greatest
"me" they can be and doesn't desire to be like others on reality TV.

A world where hard work is honored more than it is ignored. A world where all children have a home to come to.

A world where there are no lost girls and boys. A world without crime, or it rarely exists. A world where children aren't classified as misfits.

A world where people own up to their mistakes and say . . . "It was me who did it."

Still Dreaming

THE WORLD CAN BE CHANGED ONE PERSON AT A TIME; ALL IT TAKES IS SOMEONE TO BE KIND.

To really be there for someone at this time.

How can we sleep when children are starving around the world?

We would rather protest and vote on a girl marrying a girl

Than vote on a way to feed the hungry children around the world.

Voting on the legalization of marijuana, instead of banning cigarettes after years of research has proven it causes cancer, first-hand and second-hand.

But it's capital, so it'll never be banned.

Let's wake up, people, and look up the bigger plan.

It's time we stop making everything about a dollar or a follower, and make it about changing our economy for a better tomorrow.

Let's push—PUSH—for world peace, create peaceful marches in the streets.

I want to follow the steps of Nelson Mandela and Betty Wright:

They showed me we don't need guns to fight,

Just our hope and dignity to make things right.

A day will come when neighbors aren't strangers, and children will play in the streets again and not be in fear or danger.

A day will come when people will be quick to love and slow to anger; and if you see someone crying, you'll console them and let them know it'll be okay. You won't just turn your back and walk away.

The world will be changed one person at time. NOW is the time!

Willingness or Willing-less?

WHERE WOULD YOU GO TO REACH YOUR DREAMS?

Would you go to a place where there is no sunshine?

What if you had to stay there for a large span of time?

Would you consider pushing forward even if you weren't falling behind?

Would you be able to do that for a large span of time.

Are you willing to lose sleep?

Are you willing to give up something you want oh so badly to get?

Are you willing to spend time away from home?

To the point of being busy and not able to answer the phone?

Are you willing to keep going, even when everyone has told you no?

Are you willing to keep the faith, just to see yourself grow?

Are you willing to follow your heart, even when your mind says stop?

Are you willing to give your dreams all you've got?

A Teaspoon of Motivation

LIVING IN A WORLD WHERE THINGS SO OFTEN CHANGE.

Sometimes for the better. Sometimes for the worst.

Take a second. Really think about this. Sometimes the worst is for the better.

We just need to open our hearts and see.

The person sitting next to you will never be "me."

Embrace the difference, because it's true.

We're living in a world that so often changes, the worst of times, and the better of times is what gets us through.

Just Think About It

Do you know what it's like to take a leap of faith?

Give your all until there's nothing left to take?

Force a smile on your face, when you know the "good" things aren't what they seem?

Give an encouraging word to someone who's always mean?

Do you know what it's like to search for your destiny?

Gave a hand to a stranger who asked "Can you help me?"

Gave without wanting nothing at all in return?

Taught someone something that you've never learned?

What if I told you, taking a leap of faith isn't about you?

What if I told you, taking a leap of faith is about the people you pull through?

Destined

WHAT ARE YOU WAITING ON TO GET UP AND GO?

Yet, you honk at someone in traffic for going too slow.

If you're waiting on someone to give you an extra push or pull,

You'll never get up and go. You want to be taller but you don't want to grow.

Or maybe you're waiting on someone to give you a tug or a hug . . .

You want to release the water, but you don't want to pull the plug.

Get up and go. Something is waiting on you.

Don't let your dreams and goals pass you.

Driven

UNDERSTANDING THE CONCEPT OF GROWTH.

Many think of it as going up or becoming better.

Sometimes it involves an understanding of things.

Sometimes growth is the concept of what it really means.

Contrary to the phrase "money is the motivation,"

Money shouldn't be the motivation. Your passion should be.

A Poem of Small Quotes

Don't take away anything just to give.
To a situation, I mean . . .
Sometimes it takes going through things to reach our dreams.

Say what you mean.
Mean what you say.
What you say, mean.
You mean, say what?

So far gone.
A long way from home.
All I can do is sing a song.
Why mope and groan?

Stay positive. You'll feel better!
Positive energy creates positive results.
Optimism can create a world of change, and feeds positive encrgy to the brain.

A Small Prayer

PUSH FORWARD, EVEN IF IT'S SLOW.

Never stop and give up, even if life is completely messed up.

Thank God for growth—where would I be without it?

God, please bless me with patience; with it my life will never be the same.

I want to truly understand everything that is going on. To be closer to patience, I'll take the long way home.

Patience with people, who don't fully understand the power of you.

God, I'm praying for patience. Make me new.

Mentorship

ASSIGNING SOMEONE TO BE A MENTOR, LIFE COACH, OR ROLE MODEL, IS A MAJOR TASK.

A person such as will motivate you through "life class."

The concept of a mentor, life coach is so major, some people will never be able to grasp.

They won't understand what it's like to have someone to look up to.

Someone who explains it's not about what you've been through,

But about where you're going to.

As a mentee, or the person on the receiving end, you don't have to be perfect to begin.

Ask your mentor . . . She or he will be able to explain more . . .

Shepherd's Tree

I want to be where God wants to be.

I know God needs me.

I have faith; God use me.

Let me have eyes like you to be able to see.

Let me have ears like you to be able to hear.

Let me have a heart like you to be able to love.

God, I want to love, like the love that comes from above.

Let me walk with my head held high, and shine your light.

God, I just want to do what's right.

God, please guide me while I build this Shepherd's Tree.

For the Love of Music

Music has paved the way for me.

Philip Philips' song HOME comforted me when I wasn't on the path to my destiny.

When I was lost and could not see, the song WAKE ME UP by Avicii is what kept me.

Helen Baylor's TESTIMONY had me at a loss for words.

Anthony Brown's song WORTH assisted me with realizing who I really was.

BREAK EVERY CHAIN always assisted me with feeling the presence of the living God.

SPIRIT FALL DOWN by Luther Barnes was on every one of my iPods.

Nico & Vinz AM I WRONG comforted me and let me know it is what it seems.

Drake and Goapele, thank you so much for CLOSER TO MY DREAMS.

Finding Happiness in the Joke

JOKE'S ON YOU. I'M JUST BEING ME. I'M NOT HIDING. I WANT THE WORLD TO SEE.

Are you afraid of me? Or are you afraid of you?

I'm not afraid to put my sins on Front Street if it's a part of my testimony.

Are you afraid of being judged? Don't be if it isn't from the man above.

Joke's on me . . . I'm looking in the mirror, expressing what I see.

Happiness can solve a lot of issues and address a lot of changes.

Happiness can cause a hurting heart to learn.

Happiness may very much be the key.

You're the lock; say, "It starts with me."

Happiness is free and easy to obtain.

Don't take happiness as a part of a game.

Happiness can assist you with resolving the issues of life.

Just remember while seeking happiness, you may experience a little pain and strife.

Fear, Guilt, and Shame

FEAR,

I won't let you stop me.

I won't let you cover my eyes so I cannot see.

I'm still going to walk through my journey.

I won't let you cover my ears so I cannot hear.

I'll listen for the voice of God and get the message very clear.

I won't let you shift me out of first gear.

Guilt,

You will not get the best of me.

I went through things to get me where I need to be.

My past is just that, and I'll own it.

I know I've grown and my present actions have shown it.

Shame,

Stay far back away from me.

I'm growing and I don't need you to hinder me.

I don't need you to see.

I'm not embarrassed.

That's why I wrote this fear, guilt and shame letter.

Searching for What's Present

AS THE WEIGHT OF THE WORLD CRUSHES DOWN,

I look around and there's no one to be found.

I look way up and I look way down, but still there isn't anyone else to be found.

I look as far left as I possibly can go, still no one.

As far right, and still no one in plain sight.

I have faith in God, so I asked him for guidance.

He informed to me to be still and sit quiet, then you'll hear.

Take heed to my voice this time, although I've always been near.

The reason for you not seeing a soul is because it's what's destined for you.

You need no one to accomplish this goal.

You've looked everywhere except in the mirror.

When you look there, that is when the vision will become clearer.

Sometimes it's best to take a step back, stop searching in the "we,"

And realize that the someone you're searching for starts with "me."

Vulnerability

AM I NOT SOMEONE TO TUNE INTO, BECAUSE MY NAME ISN'T IN FLASHING LIGHTS?

Am I not someone to listen to, because I'm not a millionaire in life?

Am I not someone to vent to, because I'm not Dr. Phil?

Am I not someone to come to, because I haven't been known for years?

Should I not be counted on, since I'm not counting thousands?

Should I not be considered blessed, even though I don't take expensive trips to islands?

Should I not be considered, because I'm being just me?

Should I not be looked at, because my backyard doesn't have a money tree?

I possess a gift from the higher power;

For the longest I suppressed my gift like a low life coward.

Afraid to be the one to step up and stand out.

Afraid to be the rain, knowing there was a drought.

I will be the one to listen to. I'll be the change you'll start to see in you.

Change for the better, concentrating on more positive things.

Processing everything appropriately, even when you're the one to blame.

Listen to these very words I'm telling you. You'll be amazed with the change in the world around you.

Am I?

AM I WRONG FOR BEING MYSELF?

Am I wrong for trying?

When I wake up and look at the morning news, I see a lot of my people dying.

Am I wrong for caring?

Am I wrong for wanting change?

Or should I just flip the channel and say it's all one in the same?

Am I wrong for wanting more?

Am I wrong for wanting to know

The full truth behind the Trayvon story when he left the store?

Am I wrong for having doubts?

Am I wrong for worrying?

Who would I be to never have doubt and offer words of encouragement?

Am I wrong for speaking the truth?

Am I wrong for knowledge?

I'm just a black girl from the hood who graduated from college.

Am I wrong?

Don't Quit

ALL I WANT TO DO IS GIVE UP

But something is telling me I am so close

Perhaps it's time to put my pride to the side

Although I've never been the one to brag or boast

More times than not I am always more vulnerable than most

Why does success seem so imminent; can it not just be?

I am making the appropriate moves, from what I see

I encourage myself by looking in the mirror

What do I see? A person wanting to give up looking back at me

I tell myself: Reach out, maybe you'll grab your dreams

Then I wake up and those feelings aren't what they seem

I know giving up is the only way to fail

If I give up, then I'll never be able to tell

Don't give up, don't give up, and don't give up

You're way too close; one day you'll be the one to encourage most

Success is right around the corner, closer than it seems

So don't give up, you'll soon wake up

You'll soon be living your dream

Gazing

GAZING OUT OF THE WINDOWS STARING INTO THE STARS

Wondering why my dreams are near but seem so far.

Are we really who we say we are?

Sometimes it feels like my body is here on earth but my brain is on Mars

Have you ever felt lost before?

It makes you search for the truth more and more

I'm lusting after the truth, so what . . . call me a whore.

It's the ninth inning and I don't even know the score

Makes me think, what am I even here for?

Then other days I wake up and see my dream

And I get the feeling things really are what they seem

Question

One thing I've learned about age is that it doesn't bring wisdom.

Age simply brings . . . well, age.

Wisdom is gained through experience.

The experience of handling life's mishaps and exciting moments.

Age is just another way to measure things, another number.

Wisdom is knowledge, and knowledge comes with experience.

Age is just another way to tell someone: it's too late.

When wisdom tells someone: it's never too late.

Age is just another way to tell someone: you're too young.

THE JOURNEY

But knowledge lets them know: age doesn't have anything to do with it.

Learning about life's obstacles poses the intent of wisdom . . .

Are you making sound decisions?

Are your actions in good judgment?

A one year old knows not to place his hand in a fire.

Should the infant be considered wise?

A police officer received a speeding ticket on the way to work today.

Is he unknowledgeable about the consequence?

Or is this just simply a learning experience?

Should his action be considered good judgment?

Should he be considered wise?

One thing I've learned about life is that it's not about your age.

It's about YOU!

Choices

WE CHOOSE TO BE CHRISTIAN, MUSLIM, HINDU, OR A JEW.

You can't place someone in a hell you've never been to.

Or wait, I'm sorry. I'm assuming . . . Have you?

Why are we religious?

Are we not all God's children?

I think the greater power loves us equally the same.

The human race has placed labels on things,

Which causes a lot of violence. We're the ones to blame.

We can't pray in school. Or talk about God.

What's the big deal? What is there to hide?

We choose to be Christian, Muslim, Hindu, or a Jew.

The Journey

Do we choose to be confused, too?

Or wait, I'm sorry. I'm assuming . . . Are you?

Why aren't there religion courses in high school?

Is God not a major part in our lives?

Sometimes I feel like religion has to go in disguise.

We as a society have made it this way.

War on religion? We all should pray.

We should live united as a human race.

So what if my neighbors are Buddhist. The higher power wanted them that way.

We choose to be Christian, Muslim, Hindu, or a Jew.

Labeling one another as if we're perfect. And all the while, we're getting labeled, too.

Just Think

THEY NEVER SEE ME . . .

They're legally blind, but I cannot see.

She's a double amputee, but she's walking with me.

He has no arms, but he's writing his life story.

I look into her blind eyes and tell her, do not worry.

She said slow down and stop living your life in such a hurry.

Then she tells me, although I cannot see,

It's you who failed to understand.

Because of your eyes, you've been corrupted by land.

Changing yourself because of others opinions.

Utilize your gift and your real supporters; they'll listen.

THE JOURNEY

As of today, like the blind,

I challenge you to think outside the box.

I challenge you to always be yourself and never stop . . .

Change

THE ONLY THING THAT INSPIRES ME IS CHANGE.

The change for better.

The change for growth.

The change when success doesn't seem so close.

Change: noticing the good in all of the bad.

Change: finding out why you won even when you've finished last.

How to find a smile when deep down inside you're very sad.

The only thing that inspires me is change.

Complaints

COMPLAIN ABOUT LIFE AND HOW TOUGH IT IS. EVEN THOUGH YOU THANK GOD FOR BEING WHO HE IS.

Complain about a change that hasn't changed in years. Why are we still shedding the same tears?

Complain about something that happened last week. As if you're going back in time. If we could, that would be deep . . .

Complain about your job and how horrible it is. Even though it's the way you're feeding your kids.

Complain about your car being old. Even though it's getting you where you need to be.

Complain about life not being complete. What more do we need to see?

Complain about not having money to do things. When time is free.

Complain about nothing . . . While complaining about everything.

Complain about the obvious. Instead of making an obvious change.

Complain about complaining. Because I want to complain, too.

Not seeing the pain complaining is causing to the people around you . . .

Thoughts

CAN I GET LOST IN MY WORDS?

Away from this crooked world.

This world is filled with so many lies.

So many people living in disguise.

Hiding from their true self.

Focused on the money but not the wealth.

How do you do that? Look at yourself.

Men will throw thousands of dollars at females in the club,

But see their child's mother struggling and won't show her any love.

Always in the club in VIP.

But won't give a meal to a homeless person laying out on the street.

Selling dope to your mother, aunties and your people in the hood,

Then ride around on your rims and say you're living good,

While your family is the mirror of the itsy bitsy spider.

You can't even pick up the phone and let go of a grudge and tell your brother you got 'em.

We all want to reach success and make it out the 'hood.

We all want to call our mom's and let her know we about to be living good.

Instead we're like crabs in a bucket. Doing whatever we can to make it to the top.

Killing each other and robbing each other . . . Being convicted of killing your own blood brother.

The LOVE of money is the root of all sorts of wickedness. Got your neighbor's daughter killed and you had to witness it.

A five year old lying dead in the street. A bullet was the last thing to hear her heart beat.

Meanwhile her mother was twerking on the next street. Her dad was getting high laying over the bathroom sink.

THE JOURNEY

It's time to wake up, world; there's more important things than a girl marrying a girl.

There's children starving. Can I get away from this political world?

I knock no one for their success, but 100 million dollar contracts and you're flashing national debt.

Get an education is what "they say," but get in a lifetime of debt to do so.

Why is it that way? Why is it that no one has anything to say?

Maybe the debt amount is pushing people away.

Go to a university for four years to earn a degree.

Graduate and can't find a job. Forced to have insurance or be penalized.

Wake up, everyone. Open your eyes.

Get away from this tragic world.

The Love From a Woman

LOVING HARD IS WHAT WOMEN ARE TAUGHT TO DO.

Raise children, all the while we're raising men, too.

We're taught not to leave them no matter what they put us through.

They commit physical abuse, mental abuse and call us names.

Yet and still, we're taught to love them all the same.

Keeping the hurt suppressed for the sake of the family.

Hoping that all things don't fall apart.

Living in a world where the sun is shining so bright, but yet it is so dark.

Accepting lies is what woman are taught to do.

Staying for the sake of understanding what he's been through.

We're taught as women to love a man no matter what.

Even if the relationship has failed and there is zero trust.

When married, we're taught to love, honor and obey.

Even after we recognize the games men play.

Crying so many tears, for so many years.

Why can't men just be sincere?

About the Author

DENESHA DEGRAFFENREID, also known as "Journey" is a 27-year-old poetess. She is the oldest of five children and noticed her passion for writing in the 3rd grade. Journey's favorite subject in school was English. She obtained a Bachelor's Degree in Liberal Studies from the University of South Carolina with a concentration in Criminal Justice and Sociology. Later Journey decided to further her education and received a Masters of Social Work Degree from University of South Carolina. Journey has a strong desire to encourage others through words which led her to writing a poetry book titled The Journey. Denesha hopes that this book of poems has motivated, inspired, or encouraged you to keep striving for greatness throughout your life. She resides in Lancaster, South Carolina.

www.ingramcontent.com/pod-product-compliance
Lightning Source LLC
Chambersburg PA
CBHW061500040426
42450CB00008B/1431